Sharks

Written by Ben Hubbard

Collins

Sharks are the fearless hunters of the sea.

They prowl around the deep blue sea, and hunt for food.

Some sharks swim in the tropics.
There, the sea is not too hot or too cool.

Some sharks like freezing seas.

Some sharks travel around to seek out food.

Some sharks have a green hue. Some are brown, or blue with spots.

Some sharks look a bit like hammers.

Sharks have fins and tails to help them swim with speed.

fins

tail

They have strong mouths and teeth to crunch up food.

Some sharks have mouths full of sharp teeth like little daggers.

When each tooth drops out, a fresh tooth forms.

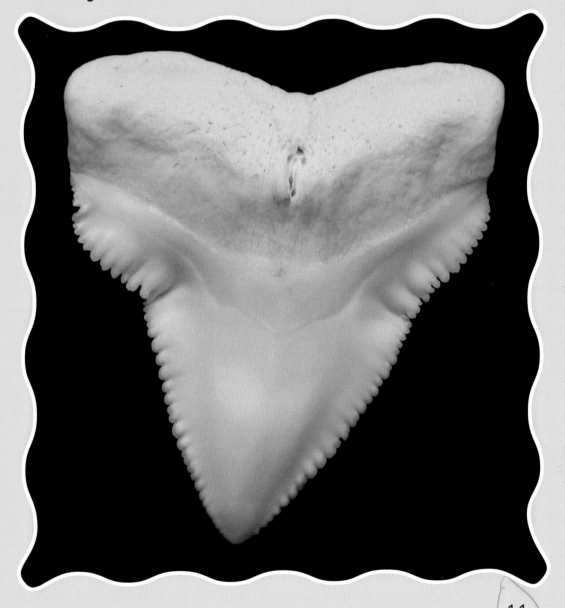

A snooping shark can push its snout around to test if it has found food.

Then it zooms up to eat the little fish!

In the day, some sharks lie in wait in the deep sea.

They swim nearer to the beach at night, to hunt.

15

Frilled sharks are deep sea sharks.

They stay down near the sea bed.

17

Sharks can lie in wait or swim around looking for food to scoop up.

If a shark fin appears in the sea, it is best to go back to the beach.

Lots of sharks are trapped in nets.
This means the number of sharks is
getting less each year.

20

Do not fear sharks. They are not monsters. They need to stay free, swimming and feeding under the sea.

Sharks

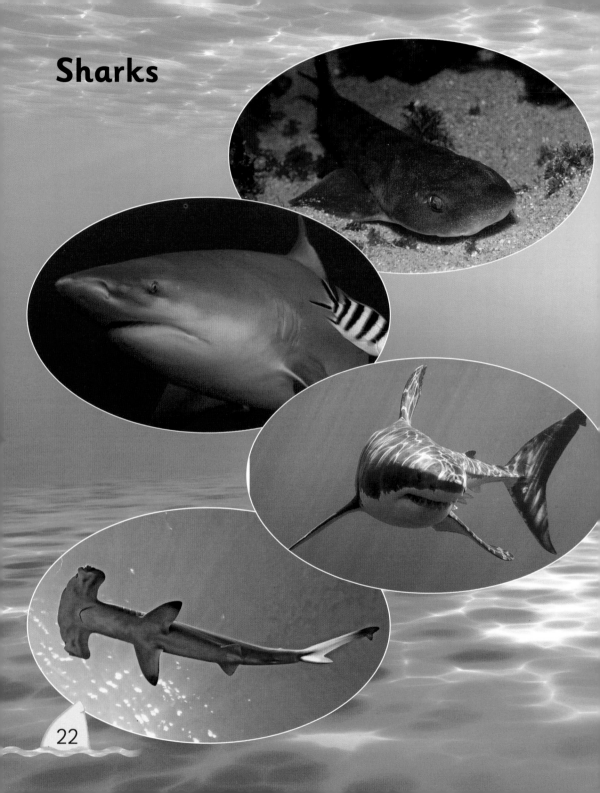

Review: After reading

Use your assessment from hearing the children read to choose any GPCs, words or tricky words that need additional practice.

Read 1: Decoding

- Look through the book. Challenge the children to find words that have the /ee/ sound in them. (*sea, speed, freezing, green, teeth, beach, deep, means*)
- How many words can they think of that rhyme with **blue**? (e.g. *true, glue*)

Read 2: Prosody

- Choose two double page spreads and model reading with expression to the children. Ask the children to have a go at reading the same pages with expression.
- Show the children how you read with authority and enthusiasm, as if you are a shark expert taking people on a deep sea tour.

Read 3: Comprehension

- Turn to pages 22 and 23. Ask children to use the pictures to help them tell you what they have found out about sharks.
- For every question ask the children how they know the answer. Ask:
  - What do sharks use their tails for? (*to help them swim*)
  - When a shark tooth falls out what happens? (*another one grows*)
  - Which type of shark did you find most interesting? Why?

23